Operation Justice

Abhijit Naskar is the twenty-first century mind of science, whose gentle and glorious philosophical touch has enabled modern Neuroscience to effectively engage in the human society towards diminishing the ever-growing conflicts among religions. As an untiring advocate of global harmony and peace, he became a beloved best-selling author all over the world with his very first book "The Art of Neuroscience in Everything". With various of his pioneering ventures into the Neuropsychology of religious sentiments, he has hugely contributed in the eradication of religious differences in our world, for which he is popularly hailed as a humanitarian neuroscientist, who takes the human civilization in the path of sweet general harmony.

OPERATION
JUSTICE

To Make A Society That
Needs No Law

ABHIJIT NASKAR

Operation Justice: To Make A Society That Needs No Law

Copyright © 2019 Abhijit Naskar

This is a work of non-fiction

An Amazon Publishing Company, 1st Edition, 2019

Printed in The United States of America

ISBN: 9781698285245

Build Bridges not Walls: In the name of Americana
The Constitution of The United Peoples of Earth
Lives to Serve Before I Sleep
When Humans Unite: Making A World Without Borders
All For Acceptance
Mission Reality
Citizens of Peace: Beyond The Savagery of Sovereignty

To All The Incorruptible
Officers of Law

CONTENTS

Understanding Justice and Order

ABHIJIT NASKAR

When a world dreams of becoming just and humane, despite being infested with injustice, discrimination, egotism and bigotry, it rather childishly attempts to instill those virtues into its members, by creating various illusive psychological structures or patterns or systems. Earlier in our ancient times, the most dominant of those structures was the structure of orthodox religion, which attempted to provide a guideline of right human behavior for all walks of life.

However, slowly, another sub-structure began to grow alongside the primary structure of religious orthodoxy, it was called law. And it came to existence, while being completely reliant on the predominant societal structure of religion, but slowly, as human intellect began to break free from the bounds of religious orthodoxy or fundamentalism towards a more secular society, the structure of law as well slowly began to function independently without any interference from religion.

And in time, this structure of law started to replace religion all together in the civilized parts of the world, as the primary guiding structure of the society. As a result, unlike our ancient days, when the humans were obligated to abide by every instructions of religion, today, a person may or not follow the orthodox religious methods, but he or she is obligated to follow the instructions of law, without any exception.

And the primary purpose of this structure of law, or simply "law", is to ensure justice in the human society - at least, that's what it is supposed to do theoretically. But when we go deeper to understand the very nature of justice, we would find that justice can never be bound or ensured with illusive psychological structures, such as law or religion or any other - especially because, all these structures are born from the fear of injustice - they are born from insecurity - and fear and insecurity breed only more fear and insecurity, not order and justice.

So, in an attempt to ensure justice, the system of law ends up creating more injustice. Punishing injustice may put a temporary halt to violence, cruelty and injustice in the society, but it doesn't actually instill justice in the society in the long run - it only makes people feel that there is justice around them, due to the lack of injustice for a short while, which is caused due to the fear of punishment, not by a genuine sense of true psychological justice.

Let's ask this question. What is justice - not the kind that you hear on the news all the time, but real, practical, genuine justice?

Here, you must not confuse law with justice, for the presence of law implies the presence of injustice, not justice. Courts exist because people have naively accepted their authority in the domain of the illusive system called "law", just like people have naively accepted the authority of the church or other religious institution in the illusive domain of faith.

But the moment, the human society begins to realize the foundational fallacies of this so-called law, all courts will crumble. I call this "law" illusive, because it is born from books known as "constitutions", which were written by lay people, on the basis of pure guess work and out of fear of chaos. And until all the constitutions of all the nations of the world go through rigorous scrutiny on the basis of facts and reason, no law born from such constitution can construct a just society.

What you call law is essentially the need of an uncivilized and unfree society. A truly civilized and free society needs no law. The presence of law is not the sign of order, but it is the sign of disorder. Hence, the true purpose of law should not be to maintain order, rather it should be to create a truly lawless society. Order lies in lawlessness, whereas in law lies disorder. So, does this mean, we should get rid of law all together!

Law is an illusory perceptual structure, a pattern, built by humans to depict the acceptable and non-acceptable behavior of humans in a certain society. This structure defines for all humans in a specific society, what is right and what is wrong. Now the question is, on what grounds does law define the righteousness of its own depictions!

Lawmakers, who rarely have an insight of a truly progressive and civilized society, decide on the perimeters of law based on their biases and knacks, and rarely on actual scientific evidence. It's like asking the blind to show the path. So, for law to be of actual use in the society at our current evolutionary stage, it must be cooked in the vessel of scientific findings with the fire of reasoning and compassion.

I'm ashamed to say that, law of today creates, not a society of order, but a society of controlled chaos. Currently law doesn't run a nation, it tactfully manages only to keep it at a standstill. Running a nation means evolving, whereas, society today hardly cares to evolve, in fact, it tries its best to hold on to its traditions, to its cultural habits, in a bone crunching attempt to resist all change, good or bad. That's why even the atrocities in our ancestors' habits and routines do not appear to us as atrocities, but only as idiosyncrasies. And that's why, injustice gets ignored by the society at large. So, though our society is called human society, it's still an animal society, and in the kingdom of the animals, injustice has always been the way of life. In the wild world, all that matters is a creature's tenacity to survive, even at the cost of harming others.

As a result, though democracy is proudly advocated across the world as, for the people, by the people, of the people, in practice, it's actually to rule the people, and squeeze their lifeforce for the benefit of those in power. And this is also the reason, why corruption prevails, because corruption is the natural way of life - crime is the natural way of life - aggression and conflicts are the natural way of life. So, just because the humans are used to feel, think and behave in a certain manner, doesn't mean that it belongs in a civilized and non-animal world that we are building - even if, the law or the government or the constitution approves of such thought, feeling and behavior, either willingly or simply by choosing to ignore it.

Government is not devoid of flaws, law is not devoid of flaws, constitution is not devoid of flaws - because the human society that gave rise to all these societal apparatus in an attempt to build a civilized world, was itself in the making. And the fact of the matter is, we still are in the making. We may call ourselves human, but we are yet to become one.

Do you know who is a human? Every creature that doesn't walk away at the sight of injustice, is a human. Every creature that doesn't look the other way, when faced with corruption, is a human. Every creature that doesn't turn a deaf ear to discrimination, is a human. Are you a human? Ask, ask and ask again, until the human in you, can't help but come out for the betterment of the society. And when it does, that will be the real dawn of true practical justice.

Justice is not a matter for only the courts to decide - justice is the responsibility for every creature that calls itself a human. Responsibility towards society automatically gives birth to justice without all the mind-boggling interventions of the law. Justice is your responsibility, it is my responsibility, it is the responsibility of each human and every human.

Here, some may most intelligently proclaim, that how can a civilian take law into their own hands? So, let me elaborate. There is a difference between taking law into your own hands and standing up to injustice. Indifference to injustice is the same as promoting an injustice, if people like to call themselves human. As I have said countless times in my previous works, to look like human is not the same as being human. To be human, is to act human, and to act human, is to stand up to all forms of inhumanity. If you don't, then I'm afraid, you are no more human than the animals in the jungle.

A human without a strong sense of justice, is no human - a human without a strong sense of acceptance, is no human - a human without a strong sense of egalitarianism, is no human. Here some may say, *"I have a family to take care of - I can't just stand up to every injustice that I encounter in the society"*. That's indeed a valid point, but let me point out to you what happens when you do not step up. You may think that indifference to injustice is the best and safest way to live in a society, but in reality, by doing so, you are actually contributing to the erection of a society that'll force your children and their children to face injustice and inequality in every walk of their life.

Their future depends on your action. You have to decide today, whether you will give them a discriminatory and unjust future by staying indifferent, or an inclusive and just future by stepping up. Wake up you must, and step up you must, not should, but must, for only then, can an animal world be changed into a human world.

Yesterday I was stupid, so I wanted to change the world. Today, I am more stupid, so I am changing the world. And tomorrow there will be a hundred more stupid like me, for this stupidity for changing the world can never accept any excuse for inaction, even if that excuse happens to be a most rational reason.

I don't care for wisdom, I don't care for knowledge, because without action, without practice, without actual realization, all wisdom, all knowledge are worthless. So, don't chase wisdom, chase action, by being the action yourself, and wisdom will follow you wherever you go. Remember, only fools talk about wisdom, the wise knows to keep silent and let their action do the talking.

The world is waiting, to celebrate you with love.

All you gotta do, is lose yourself and be a dove.

Lose all maps, and walk in service beyond convention.

Only then will you gain glory, only then will you have emancipation.

Justice is Human Matter,
Not Legal Matter

A few words mumbled by a judge, ain't going to ensure justice in the society, what will, is a genuine sense of responsibility towards the society in each one of us. When enough humans in the society are responsible towards their society, injustice as a way of life, will slowly turn into a matter of yesteryear. And this can begin only with you, you the individual, regardless of whether you are a bureaucrat, a cop, an attorney, a politician or a civilian.

It is this simple, society is the responsibility of the citizens, each citizen, every citizen - the bureaucrat is a citizen, the judge is a citizen, the cop is a citizen, the politician is a citizen, the civilian is a citizen. We all are citizens, the question is, are we human citizens or animal citizens?

Animals are the citizens of the organic jungle, humans are the citizens of the inorganic jungle. Now, to call this inorganic jungle a civilized, sentient and conscientious society, the humans must first learnt to act civilized, sentient and conscientious. The question is, do the so-called "humans" act human? If they do, then perhaps, we can move forward to understand what justice has to do with law, if anything.

Justice is not a legal matter, it's a human matter. It's a matter for every human to be concerned with. If they are not, then they have no right to call themselves human. In fact, justice and humanity are not different, they are one and the same thing - where there is justice, there is humanity - where there is no humanity, there is no justice.

A society of humans means a just society, if not, then it's not a human society in the first place. However, this doesn't mean that such a society would be absolutely devoid of injustice and cruelty, rather it simply means that, in a human society, acts of justice outweigh acts of injustice - acts of kindness outweigh acts of cruelty – acts of acceptance outweigh acts of discrimination. Justice doesn't mean absence of injustice, it means the presence of human will to stand up to injustice. And this will is not the exclusive possession of only one profession called the "law", rather it's the universal faculty of every living, breathing, civilized and conscientious human being.

Also, some so-called practical people may say, it's idiotic for a civilian to try to stand up to the injustice in the society. This is a rather valid point, so let's go slow here. Indeed there are certain circumstances of injustice, that are better left to the officers of the law, such as in event of armed aggression and violence. But except for these extreme situations, most of the injustice in the society are committed by ordinary people, who can commit them because no one in the society feels responsible enough to stand up to them.

Such injustice can come in all shapes and sizes. A lawman asking for bribe from a civilian to fulfill certain necessary paperwork, is committing injustice. A pervert who gropes and manhandles a woman in public transportation, is committing injustice. A college student who bullies the newcomers, is committing injustice. These are the injustice committed by ordinary people that occur around the world on a daily basis, all because the people around are either afraid or do not feel responsible enough to stand up to them. If they did, if you do, if only a handful of individuals in every corner of the society stand up to such everyday injustice, then we will witness a revolutionary decline in the very graph of crime and chaos all over the world.

Here, I give you the golden principle of justice today - injustice is bound to drop in proportion to rising social responsibility - poverty is bound to drop in proportion to rising social responsibility - discrimination and inequality are bound to drop in proportion to rising social responsibility. So, all it takes, to build a humane world, a compassionate world, an accepting and empathetic world, is a sense of genuine responsibility towards one's society.

I am not asking you to give up everything and go out to work for the society, though such sacrifice is indeed necessary, at least, by a handful of individuals, all I am asking is do your part in your daily walks of life, and make whatever difference you can in your corner of the world. It is this simple, when you see an act of injustice taking place in front of your eyes, don't walk away - stand up.

What's the point of all your intellect, and smartness and so-called decency, if you don't have the basic guts to stop an injustice from happening in your vicinity! Forget the world, forget civilization, forget all those pompous ideas of progress and global goals, simply take a stand in your vicinity, in your locality, against discrimination, against prejudices, against corruption and harassment.

Global goals are futile, if the individual human doesn't take responsibility for the issues of his or her own neighborhood. Change in the world begins with change in your neighborhood. And change in your neighborhood begins with change in you - a change from indifference to responsibility - a change from purpose-less survival to purpose-full living.

Before writing a book, I think about the purpose that the book would serve in the society, sometimes for weeks, sometimes months, and sometimes for about a year. Once I have a clear insight of the purpose, then the words automatically start flowing from my mind onto the page. In short, if you have a purpose, action flows on its own, but if you don't have a purpose, then no matter how much you try to keep busy, at the end of the day, you end up achieving nothing. So, find the purpose of life, and give your all to that purpose - let that purpose spread through your actions like an epidemic.

Become an epidemic, o my brave soldier of time, an epidemic of acceptance, an epidemic of kindness and sacrifice, an epidemic of justice and egalitarianism, an epidemic that is untreatable and incurable. Only then, our mission for justice, equality and universal unification will witness the first dawn of real civilization, a civilization beyond bigotry, beyond segregation and beyond mystical fraudulence.

How can you be relaxed, my friend - when mystics, spiritualists, fundamentalists and transhumanists keep conning people - when the politicians (not all) keep conning people - when the bureaucrats (not all) keep conning people - when the very system of democracy keeps conning people, by depriving them of the faculty of reason, inclusion and thought? Is this modern - is this civilized - is this human? Think.

Think with all your nature-given potential of thought and become restless - become restless for action - become restless for change - and not just any change, but become restless for a humane change - a change that instills justice in law - a change that instills reason and merit in government and administration - a change that instills humanity in the human society.

I am restless 24/7. No matter how much I do for the world, it never feels enough, it never feels as if I have done something substantial. Become restless my friend, not for romance, not for sex, not for fame, money or reputation, but for making the contribution of change in the society, with your thoughts, with your emotions, with your actions, with your whole being.

The world needs not new governments - the world needs not new parties - the world needs not new dictators masquerading as leaders or entrepreneurs - what the world needs is thought, punned in the flames of reason, courage and humaneness. Politics is not going to save this world, science and technology are not going to save this world, religion and spirituality are not going to save this world - what will is our understanding of which belongs where and to what extent.

Understanding empowers action – it strengthens the mind to break free from the shackles of meekness induced toleration. Tolerate no bigotry, tolerate no discrimination, tolerate no injustice, cruelty and hate. In a free society, people may be entitled to their belief, but they are not entitled to bigotry. To the bigots, this may seem like tyranny, but it's an absolute necessity, just like it is absolutely imperative that psychopathic murderers are kept off the streets.

For example, a mentally broken serial killer may say, they are entitled to kill people if they desire so, because it's a free society. A perverted bully may say, they are entitled to grab women by their vagina, because it's a free society. A mindless bigot may say, they are entitled to spread the word of supremacy of their own religion and scripture over all others, because it's a free society. But all such behaviors, thoughts and opinions belong in the jungle, not in a society, that's ought to be civilized, that's ought to be conscientious and that's ought to be safe and hateless.

If an amendment ensures such right to expression, then the amendment needs to change - if a policy ensures such a right to expression, then the policy needs to change - if a system of law ensures such a right to expression, then that very system has to be changed. Bigotry, hate, bullying, perversion and discrimination must never be considered to be human rights, because if we do, then we will never in a million years be able to instill real justice, equality and acceptance in the human society.

Freedom to practice one's own religion, doesn't mean belittling other religions. Freedom to practice one's own belief, doesn't mean belittling the belief of others. A free society means a responsible society, for if a free society is not responsible, then such society is no different from the kingdom of the wild. And a responsible society means a society, which is capable of standing up to all injustice, even if it comes from the very keepers of the law.

In The Service of Law

People love to say, nobody is above the law, which is one of the most dangerous delusions of the social psyche. It is a lie fed to the meek citizens of a nation to keep them obedient to the state, even in the face of corruption. Every human is above the law, until the law that governs the society is made incorruptible (or at least close to incorruptible).

So long as we have a law that is exploitable by individuals in power, it is imperative that every thinking human stands up to such law, even if it means going against the state, because like the law of today, state itself is not incorruptible. Any form of power has the potential to corrupt its possessor. So, ultimately it all comes down to individual responsibility – a sense of responsibility that stops a person from abusing his or her so-called power or authority.

A Judge means not authority of justice, but guardian of justice. And as such, it is imperative, that a judge never stops learning, not just about criminal psychology, but about all the obvious and subtle aspects of human nature. If a person gets appointed as a judge at a court bench and thinks that, all need for learning about justice and human nature has ended, then I am afraid, such a judge is lethal to the very administration of justice in the society. And this applies to not just a judge, but to the entire body of officials involved in the administration of law and order in the society.

If a person becomes a police officer and thinks he or she no longer needs to learn about criminology, detective work and human nature as a whole, then such a police officer is lethal to the very system of law in the society. A police should always stay updated on not just forensic sciences, but more importantly on emerging research in the fields of Neurocriminology and Neurolaw (an emerging field which helps the law to make more ethical and righteous decisions based on neurological data of an accused's brain state). And so should a judge, lawyer, attorney and every other official who's involved in the system of law, order, enforcement and justice.

Now is the time that, with the rise of new evidence in Neurocriminology, the traditional and less accurate justice system of today has a renovation - only then will we be able to deliver proper and more accurate verdicts that may essentially have an irreparable impact on people's lives.

Arrogance and egotism have no place in the justice system. People are not machines - people are organic creatures - they make mistakes - and only when they recognize those mistakes and are ready to learn from them, can then succeed not only in growing as individuals but also in carrying out their duty in the society effectively and righteously. It's not wrong to make mistakes, but to not accept those mistakes is.

A judge, an attorney, a police officer, a civilian, everyone is a living breathing human being, and as such, any of them can make a mistake. And the system of justice itself is a living breathing symposium of organic humans, so, it can't be impervious to mistakes either. But we can only construct a just society, where every individual in the justice system and the law enforcement is prepared, to admit that they are human beings like any other, and to learn and grow from and through their mistakes.

And, when the order of an entire society is on your shoulders, you do not have the luxury to stay stagnant mentally, you must grow, you must learn, you must become more and more human every single day, by gathering information on your field and related fields, and by studying them regularly to have a deeper insight into the very nature of justice. Figure out for yourself, the meaning of justice – the meaning of order – the meaning of honesty and dignity.

Bow not, my brave officer of the law, before the soul-crunching pressure of corruption – light up the nuclear furnace of responsibility and justice that sleeps dormant within you and crush all corruption to ashes – only then you'll become the very embodiment of courage, conscience and order in the human society. You are not to live for yourself, as a labor of law – you are to live in the service of humans, as the very life-force of law in the human society. You are to exist as a living, breathing incarnate of order, harmony and civilization.

Rise and act – and corruption will be afraid of you – injustice will be afraid of you – inequality will be afraid of you. And remember, you must be a friend to the people – a guide to the people – a guardian to the people – and this means, not only protecting the people against obvious anti-social activity, but more importantly it means defending the rights of the people against all forms of anti-social and corrupt behavior even if it comes from your own department or from the government officials or politicians controlling the department.

Yours is not like any other profession – upon your duty depends whether a little child in a corner of your neighborhood will sleep sound – upon your duty depends whether a woman can return home safe from work at night – upon your duty depends whether an elderly person can reach home from the bank without being mugged. You matter – your duty matters – not merely for you mark you, but for those countless civilians who rely on your individual sense of responsibility with their very life. You are to be the lion that keeps all vicious predators away when it roams the neighborhood.

You are not just a police officer, you are the caretaker of hundreds of lives. Do you feel this, my friend? Do you feel it in your bones? If you do, then simply act in the line of duty with a purifying force of conscience flowing through your veins, and justice will follow – safety will follow – order will follow. You can't maintain the law, for you are the law – you can't maintain order, for you are the order – so put on the uniform and be what you are supposed to be – the vanguard of society. The law and order within you will outpour into the society through your duty, once you become one with your duty. So, be one with your duty – be one with the society – be one with the people – and all will be well.

When a burning sense of duty flows through the veins of a police officer like blood, it turns the very word police into an emblem of hope – an emblem of righteousness – an emblem of integrity, dignity and morality. Be an officer my friend, an officer with the guts to do right to the right and right to the wrong.

Knowing what's wrong changes nothing, what does is our action to make things right. And remember, politics is not your business – bureaucracy is not your business – corporate interest is not your business – in this whole wide world, your interest is only one – and that is, protection of the people. Mark this my friend, a COP means Caretaker Of People – not of the selfish and authoritarian interests of politicians and bureaucrats.

The world doesn't need more bent police who pretend to uphold the law in front of an investigation, it needs more just police who practice justice even when nobody is looking. Here, some may say, the police may uphold justice, but they must never deliver justice.

However, that's where the current notion of justice turns infantile. Any police, who stops an injustice from happening in the society, is the real deliverer of justice, not the court. Once an injustice has occurred, the court may deliver punishment to those who committed the injustice, but delivering punishment for committing injustice, is not the same as delivering justice. Justice is the act of preventing injustice, not the act of punishing injustice. Courts do not deliver justice, they deliver either punishment or settlement.

The advocates of the so-called court system may say, punishing injustice is their way to prevent injustice from happening in the future. Here again, lawmakers make assumptions, based on absolute guess work, not unlike gamblers in the casino, that fear of punishment leads to less injustice. This may be partially true, but such a method of using punishment as a tool to prevent injustice and crime, leads to an immature, dishonest, snobbish and superficial society, that has no practical understanding of the term "justice". The most effective, civilized and psychologically healthy way to prevent injustice, is to raise a society that needs no law to maintain order and sustain justice.

Finally, to the whole body of law (police, attorneys and judges), I ask this question - do you know what justice is! Do you have any clue to the nature of justice - not the one that you are taught in school, but a genuine, self-empowering, living and breathing force for good and righteousness, which is capable enough to sustain itself, even without the intervention of authority figures of the law?

Unless you feel the force of justice moving through your veins, you haven't understood justice yet, no matter how many verdicts you have delivered or how many criminals you have jailed. It's not about taking law in your own hands, or about being a vigilante, it's about breaking free from the cocoon of indifference.

Stepping up in the face of injustice, is not vigilantism, it's humanity - and being indifferent to injustice is not smartness, it's barbarism. To ensure justice in the society, is not just the responsibility of the law, it's the responsibility of every human being on earth.

Praying for justice, praying for rights, praying for an egalitarian society won't magically make this world just, humane and egalitarian. Rights are nobody's ancestral possession to be gifted to you - you must manifest them in your footsteps and turn yourself into an indomitable, humane and titanic force of nature.

Be a regular titan of justice and equality in your plain ordinary everyday life, only then can true order begin to flow in our society. Remember, in a civilized society, law and order can never go hand in hand - only when we can create a society that needs no law to sustain order, will we have the right to call ourselves civilized - to call ourselves just - and to call ourselves human.

ABHIJIT NASKAR

Into The Land of Justice, Beyond Law

Laws, policies and amendments are not going to ensure justice in the human society, unless the humans - each human - all humans, uphold justice with utmost courage, care and conscience in their daily walks of life. And this can only happen, if you turn wise enough to see the society as a reflection of yourself. Every harm done to the society, is harm done to me - every injustice done to the society, is injustice done to me - every corruption faced by the society, is corruption faced by me. Such should be the thinking of a responsible and civilized individual of the human society.

All behavior begins with thought. Responsible thought leads to responsible behavior - and responsible behavior leads to responsible society. However, responsible thought doesn't rise simply on the foundation of loose sentimentality, it rises on the combined foundation of human sentiment and reasoning.

Justice is a human virtue, whereas law is a social construct that tries to bind that virtue in a paradigm. And to some extent, this binding – this codification may be healthy, but once the humans begin to confuse the paradigm with the virtue itself, the very fabric of social character starts to get rather thin and shallow. Justice must be realized by each human of the thinking society in their bones, only then can we create a just society, a society beyond the childish paradigm of law. A truly civilized and just society needs no law.

And we must start working right this very moment to build the law-less society. And it can only start with the children. We must start working right now to raise not law-abiding citizens, but citizens who would have the indomitable conscience and courage to stand up to every injustice in their society. We must, with our just footsteps, become the founding figures of the just society that we never had ourselves.

At our own free will, we must make this declaration to ourselves today - the declaration of justice - the declaration of order - the declaration of a united independence from the oppression of prejudices, hate and segregation.

In the course of human events, if ever, injustice grabs hold of the landscape that we the people step foot on, it will be our organically divine right to abolish such injustice, with our thoughts, words and actions conscientious. We the people, each one of us, will do our utmost to create a society that needs not the intervention of law or any specialist authority. We will create a society of humans with our own two hands for the humans that are yet to be born, so that they may know justice and order in their life, which we have been deprived of due to the indifference and callousness of our ancestors. We the living, breathing and thinking humans do solemnly declare upon our functional conscience, that from this moment onwards, we will no longer adhere to the traditional habit of dependency, hypocrisy and meekness, and we will come to the aid of every human who faces injustice in any form, with this golden principle engraved upon our hearts, that there are no foreigners, only family.

Only if we are protective of our whole humankind, the way we are protective of our own family, will there be hope for an inclusive and humane society. Society begins with the self, and as such, traits of the self become the traits of the society - nature of the self becomes the nature of the society. Now the question is, what is the nature of the self - of the human self, to be specific?

The first and foremost fact that I must point out right away on this matter, is that the nature of the human self is neither completely good nor completely evil, for in nature there is no such thing as good and evil, moral and immoral, righteous and unrighteous, acceptance and discrimination, justice and injustice, but only feats for survival.

Virtues are of little significance, if a creature is living in the wild. To survive in the wild, it has to be cruel and unrighteous. But the point is, we only see the way of life in the wild to be cruel and unrighteous, because in our mind we have developed certain notions of civilized traits - traits of kindness, ethics and righteousness.

However, this doesn't mean that animals can't be kind, rather it means that the wilderness doesn't leave much room for practicing kindness that prevails in the brain circuits of many animals in the form of empathy. An organic creature has to adapt to its environment, if it is to survive. Which means that if an environment compels a creature to be unscrupulous, then it's bound to become unscrupulous.

Therefore, if we are capable of creating an environment on the foundation of ethics, justice and humaneness - an environment that doesn't compel its residents to be unscrupulous, then the humans in it will finally have the societal space to nourish and practice the virtues that lie within them dying to see the light of day.

Now this is easier said than done - it's a serious task to be carried out by an entire generation of humans - the generation of today. And this can be achieved in two folds - by being responsible, conscientious and non-indifferent citizens of the world ourselves, and at the same time, we have to instill the same sense of responsibility and principles in our kids.

Raising the sense of responsibility and principles in our kids is simpler than you can imagine. All you have to do is spend a little time with them on a daily basis, all through their developing years. With the rise of social media, the level of empathy among the kids has diminished greatly, and if this continues due to our indifference, then I'm afraid, we'll be giving rise to a planet full of sociopaths.

So, beware of your kid's screen consumption time - it's a matter of life and death - of psychological life and psychological death. Raise them in a way that they do not lose their sense of community and their sanity amidst the fake crowd of hashtags and emojis.

Quite literally speaking, human life stands at the crossroads of sanity and insanity, and every action that we take now will have irreversible repercussions in the life of our future humanity. So, as I said in my TED Talk, "Go out into the world and act. Act with all the might in your veins. Act with all the conscience in your nerves. Act beyond all dogmas, doctrines and discriminations, so that the humanity of tomorrow will be grateful to you for delivering them a world of acceptance, a world of humaneness, and above all, a world of a unified progressive humankind."

Throw away all indifference, throw away all callousness, throw away all meekness and stand up. Once you stand up, the world will stand up - once you speak up, the world will speak up.

Stand up and speak up loud - "I am the pillar of justice - I am the pillar of courage - I am the pillar of honor - I am the pillar of action without rage. No injustice can brew while I am standing - no discrimination can pester while I am walking - no hate can spread while I am present - no prejudice can prevail while I am still breathing."

Justice is not a piece of pie that you can buy at the court of law - justice is the virtue that ensures that no human is deprived of their existential rights - it is the virtue that ensures that no human is discriminated in any manner based on their gender, color, religion or sexual orientation - justice is the virtue that ensures that no human feels uncomfortable or unaccepted while standing amidst other humans - and that virtue cannot be ensured by only the illusive system of law.

It is the responsibility of each thinking and compassionate human to ensure that no corruption, no aggression and no primitiveness can take away justice from the lives of the humans around us. Only if each of us has this sense of universal justice, then can we make sure that tomorrow will be a just tomorrow for our children and for all the humans yet to be born.

In short, justice is not a gift to be bestowed upon us by the law, it's a virtue that lives within us, and we all need to make conscientious efforts to make it manifest in the society. If we don't, if we simply keep on relying on the intervention of some illusive law or some illusive God, then we will spend our whole life as a species, in the darkness of injustice.

Each one of us must become a Captain Planet, taking the responsibility of our societies up on our shoulders, or else, justice, acceptance and harmony will remain a fiction till kingdom come. Each one of us is responsible for the world - each one of us must give a hand to build our world in a humane manner, crossing faith, fate and family.

It's not about social responsibility, it's plain ordinary human responsibility. In fact, there is no such thing as social responsibility, because social responsibility implies that it's an act that adds extra value to a person's humanly character, whereas in reality, without a sense of responsibility towards the society, a person is no human in the first place.

Those who make no contributions to the society, show off with cars, motorcycles, credit cards and other meaningless material possessions. The life of a human has meaning only and only if that life comes to the aid of others. And that very act of being an aid to others is the highest manifestation of justice.

Law may be complicated, being a human invention, but justice, being a natural quality, is rather simple - as simple as love or kindness. In fact, in their purest manifestation, love, kindness and justice are one and the same. Where there is love, there is justice - where there is no love, there is no justice. And love is the purest form of expectation-less kindness, hence kindness itself is justice. So, to be kind is, to be loving, and to be loving is, to be just. Call it love, call it kindness, call it spirituality, call it justice, it's all one.

The essence of all virtues is one and the same, it's love. All virtues are reflections of this one universal force of love. In fact, love is the master key to all the issues of the society. So, if you have love in your heart, and the courage in your veins to act on that love, no matter the consequence, then on injustice will have the power to raise its poisonous fangs in our society.

Love in its purest form, is devoid of all expectation, sexual or otherwise. It is pure care - not selfless mark you, for selfless implies there is no self involved, rather it's a care which saturates the self with meaning, purpose and with an absolute sense of effortless belonging - it is the highest fulfillment of the self.

Don't be selfless, be selfish, very, very selfish - selfish enough to destroy yourself, in an attempt to bring smiles on the clouded faces of our society, selfish enough to be ready to get annihilated, in an attempt to uplift the downtrodden. Be selfish, my friend - and let that selfishness grow so big that no amount of injustice, misery and discrimination can raise their arrogant heads in front of you. Let your selfishness for seeing others lifted, blow over your entire society like a whiff of rejuvenating fresh air taking away the darkness, the misery and the inequalities from even the remotest corner.

Injustice, cruelty and corruption are the usual state of our natural world - but they can only prevail in darkness, not in light - they can't bear the penetrating and purifying rays of light, of hope, of conscience and of character. So, to eliminate them from our society, or at least, to incapacitate them, we must be the penetrating rays of conscience and character ourselves - justice will come, equality will come, acceptance will come, and above all, wise, harmonious progress will come.

The Four Pillars of
Humanhood

Injustice won't destroy our world, indifference to injustice will. Be not an insect of indifference, be the godzilla of zeal and deeds. Break your sleep of silence and fear, and wake up. Wake up from death, return to life. Life is meant to be explored, not feared, so explore it with all your might and stand tall with conscience and humaneness as your backbone.

The world is crumbling - society is crumbling - humanity is stooping - not because of inhuman actions, but due to the lack of retaliation to those acts of inhumanity. Every time you face discrimination or you see someone facing discrimination, you simply walk away - why? Forget justice, forget law and order, for police, judge and court, and start by simply not walking away, if you really genuinely want a just and humane society for your children.

Break your silence, and injustice will lose strength - break your indifference, and corruption will feel weak - break your fear, and discrimination will start to shiver - break your sleep, and inhumanity will begin to weep. Just wake up and start walking, and destiny will be moulded according to your footsteps.

And, don't let the illusion of destiny keep you from doing what you love to do - for nothing is meant to be, or not to be - it is only your willful and persistent action that determines your destiny. And it's not just your destiny at stake here, it's the destiny of your society that's on the line.

It's this simple, your indifference will make way for an inhuman destiny, whereas if you muster the courage to act upon your conscience, then your action will pave the dawn of a true humane destiny. Destiny is determined by deeds, so do the deed, and pay the mockery no heed.

Determination, devotion and deliberation are the fundamental pillars of societal growth. Each individual must be determined for growth, devoted to upliftment and must have the capacity for deliberation or careful contemplation. Also, each individual must be very cautious of how he or she behaves, when nobody is watching, because your action at that very moment, is the purest reflection of your true character.

Self-observation is the highest faculty of an advanced species - a species of conscience and character. And from that very self-observation rises true insight of not just justice, but of the actual functionings of a peaceful and progressive society. To create a just and progressive society, you must first see it manifesting in your mind, plain as day, and when you do, you won't be able to hold yourself from working to make that vision a reality.

And do not even for a second, think of this vision to be mere imagination - it is much more than that - it is beyond imagination - vision is imagination fueled by an indomitable force of determination, dedication and courage. If you have a genuine exuberant vision of a just and humane society, then no obstacle is strong enough to be an impediment in your path.

In the jungle, animals ravage each other for survival, and no thinking human should intervene to stop it, because kill or be killed is the law of survival in the wild - so by intervening you may stop a few animals from killing each other for a short while, but after you are gone, they will start killing each other again, since they are neurologically and environmentally incapable of a non-cruel alternative.

But when humans kill each other in a civilized society for exclusive supremacy or for any other primitive reason, a thinking human must intervene, because civilized society is not ought to be run by the wild law of kill or be killed, it is ought to be run by the humane principles of acceptance and equality, because though we humans find it easier to fight each other for illusive reasons, since it has been the way of life for our wild ancestors, later in our not so distant evolutionary past we the human species alone developed the neurological capacity to look beyond the savage desire for personal survival.

A handful of thinking bravehearts in every corner of the world must stand up to empower the capacity for acceptance and egalitarianism within the humans around them, so that slowly but surely, the civilized traits of justice, order and peace triumph over our primitive traits of discrimination, aggression and prejudices.

Remember, there are two kinds of creatures in the world, those who stand by and watch injustice happen, and those who stand up to stop an injustice from happening. The former are spine-less insects, the latter are humans. What are you? And if you feel offended, by this statement in any manner, or disrespected, then it implies that you are not responsible of your society, and if you are not responsible, you are not human in the first place.

But if you have the torch of responsibility burning in your heart, then with that torch, light up your vision of an actual human society that not only looks human, but acts human, and live that vision with every drop of blood in your veins and every spark of electricity in your nerves.

You have to decide right now, in which direction you want to take the society. And do not think of this to be some gargantuan task, all you have to do is, think feel and act human as you walk through your day. You don't have to give all your savings to some charity to make this world a humane and just place, rather you just need to give a little hand whenever and wherever you see someone in need.

Wherever there is injustice, there is scope for being human - wherever there is cruelty, there is scope for being human - wherever there is discrimination, there is scope for being human. So, be human, in every sense of the term, not just in theory. There is a vast difference between theory and practice. In theory, you may think you are human, but you ain't a human, unless you come to the aid of other humans in need. To elaborate this further, here I give you four foundational pillars of being human - four pillars of humanhood.

The four pillars of humanhood are devotion, duty, acceptance and action - devotion to human interest, duty to stand up to discrimination, bigotry and injustice, acceptance of all humans regardless of belief, intellect and status, and action to eliminate the issues in one's society.

And these are nothing theoretical for you to memorize and then try to abide by them, like the religious fundamentalists abide by the words of their scriptures. Rather, they are common human characteristics that manifest in a human quite naturally, once that human recognizes and realizes his or her true communion with the society - true oneness with the society.

All action comes from realization. It is the mother of all change. When you realize that you are responsible, you no longer need to think about how to act, you no longer need to make efforts to act, rather real, practical action drives your whole being. In realization being and action merge into one eternal, ever-purifying force of upliftment. In upliftment lies justice - in upliftment lies order - in upliftment lies harmony - in upliftment lies civilization.

What is upliftment? Is there any persistent and non-changing meaning or nature or measure of upliftment? Can there even be any single purpose behind the term upliftment? Can over seven billion humans ever agree on any one mission of upliftment? Is upliftment yet another illusive utopian idea?

In response to all these wonderings, allow me to ask you only two questions - what are you and how big is your family? In practice, real tangible upliftment takes place in the lives of your family, without you or them even giving any thought to the term upliftment - that's because you are there for your family - you stand by them through all storms - you stand by them no matter their mistakes - you stand by them regardless of their occasional criticisms of you - you stand by them, through suffering, joy, failures and achievements. Likewise, once the illusory boundary of our immediate family lifts from our psyche, upliftment is bound to take place in the society, whether we are even familiar with the term upliftment or not.

Upliftment of the society is bound to happen, all you need to do is take the necessary steps yourself to counter the troubles of your society, instead of relying on the intervention of some law, judge or god. Bring such an earthquake of change with your actions that even the richter scale breaks into pieces. Enough predators are walking free in our society, not unlike in the jungle, because law of today is not incorruptible - and for it to actually become incorruptible, each human being of the society must become the embodiment of justice. Justice, liberty and acceptance must flow through our veins as lifeblood.

To bring up an excerpt from my work "When Humans Unite",

"The world needs madness, a madness for justice, a madness for harmony, a madness for equality, a

madness for humanitarian glory. If everyone had the madness for doing good, there wouldn't be any misery in the world. So, be mad, be furious, be rebellious towards every bit of misery, inequality and injustice in the world. Remember, every injustice anywhere in the world is your business, every misery anywhere in the world is your business, every segregation anywhere in the world is your business. Human condition anywhere in the world is your business."

Think for a while, if one species can force an entire planet to get warmer with their reckless actions, can they also not create a just, humane and loving society with their responsible actions! They can - you can - we can - and we must - we must do the needful, not next month, not next week, not tomorrow, but we must start living as bold and conscientious beings of action, from this moment onwards.

Bibliography

Archer M., (2000), Being Human: The Problem of Agency. Cambridge University Press.

Archer M., (2003), Structure, Agency and the Internal Conversation. Cambridge University Press.

Adolphs R (2003) Cognitive neuroscience of human social behaviour. Nature Rev Neurosci 4: 165–178.

Adolphs R, Tranel D, Damasio AR (2003) Dissociable neural systems for recognizing emotions. Brain Cogn 52: 61–69.

Afton, A. D. (1985). Forced copulation as a reproductive strategy of male lesser scaup: A field test of some predictions. - Behaviour 92, p. 146-167.

Allison T, Puce A, McCarthy G. (2000) Social perception from visual cues: role of the STS region. Trends Cogn Sci 4: 267–278.

Andresen, Jensine, and Robert Forman, eds. Cognitive Models and Spiritual Maps. Bowling Green, Ohio: Imprint Academic, 2000.

Ashbrook, James, and Carol Albright. The Humanizing Brain: Where Religion and Neuroscience Meet. Cleveland, OH: Pilgrim Press, 1997.

Azari, Nina, Janpeter Nickel, Gilbert Wunderlich, Michael Niedeggen, Harald Hefter, Lutz Tellmann, Hans Herzog, Petra Stoerig, Dieter Birnbacher, and Rudiger Seitz. "Neural Correlates of Religious Experience." European Journal of Neuroscience 13, no. 8 (2001)

Agar, N. (2004). Liberal eugenics: In defence of human enhancement. London: Blackwell Publishing.

Alteheld, N., Roessler, G., Vobig, M., & Walter, R. (2004). The retina implant new approach to a visual prosthesis. Biomedizinische Technik, 49(4), 99–103.

Antal, A., Nitsche, M. A., Kincses, T. Z., Kruse, W., Hoffmann, K. P., & Paulus, W. (2004a). Facilitation of visuo-motor learning by transcranial direct current stimulation of the motor and extrastriate visual areas in humans. European Journal of Neuroscience, 19(10), 2888–2892.

Bhat Z, Kumar, S, Bhat H (2015) In vitro meat production. Challenges and benefits over conventional meat production. J Sci Food Agric 14: 241–248

Bernstein R. J., (1967), John Dewey. New York: Washington Square Press.

Bernstein R.J., (1971), Praxis and Action: Contemporary Philosophies of Human Activity. Philadelphia: University of Pennsylvania Press.

Bernstein R.J., (1976), The Restructuring Social and Political Thought.

Bernstein R.J., (1983), Beyond Relativism and Objectivism: Science, Hermeneutics, and Praxis. Philadelphia: University of Pennsylvania Press.

Bernstein R.J., (1986), Philosophical Profiles. Philadelphia: University of Pennsylvania Press.

Bernstein R.J., (1991), New Constellation. Cambridge: MIT Press.

Barash, D. P. (1977). Sociobiology of rape in mallards (Anas platyrhynchos): Responses of the mated male. - Science 197, p. 788-789.

Berger, J. (1986). Wild horses of the great basin: Social competition and population size. - The University of Chicago Press, Chicago.

Birkhead, T. R., Johnson, S. D. & Nettleship, D. N. (1985). Extra-pair matings and mate guarding in the common murre Uria aalge. - Anim. Behav. 33, p. 608-619.

Beauregard, Mario, and Vincent Paquette. "Neural Correlates of a Mystical Experience in Carmelite Nuns." Neuroscience Letters 405, no. 3 (2006)

Benson, Herbert. Timeless Healing: The Power and Biology of Belief. New York: Scribner, 1996

Bogen, J.E.(1995a), 'On the neurophysiology of consciousness: Part I. An overview', Consciousness and Cognition, 4.

Bogen, J.E. (1995b), 'On the neurophysiology of consciousness: Part II. Constraining the semantic problem', Consciousness and Cognition, 4.

Bremner, J. D., R. Soufer, et al. (2001). "Gender differences in cognitive and neural correlates of remembrance of emotional words." Psychopharmacol Bull 35 (3).

Brothers, L. (2002). The social brain: A project for integrating primate behavior and neurophysiology in a new domain. In J. T. Cacioppo et al. (Eds.), Foundations in neuroscience. Cambridge, MA: MIT Press.

Buss, D. D. (2003). Evolutionary Psychology: The New Science of Mind, 2nd ed. New York: Allyn & Bacon.

Buss, D. M. (1989). "Conflict between the sexes: Strategic interference and the evocation of anger and upset." J Pers Soc Psychol 56 (5).

Buss, D. M. (1995). "Psychological sex differences. Origins through sexual selection." Am Psychol 50 (3).

Buss, D. M. (2002). "Review: Human Mate Guarding." Neuro Endocrinol Lett 23 (Suppl 4).

Buss, D. M., and D. P. Schmitt (1993). "Sexual strategies theory: An evolutionary perspective on human mating." Psychol Rev 100 (2).

Blakemore SJ, Decety J (2001) From the perception of action to the understanding of intention. Nature Rev Neurosci 2: 561.

Bruce C, Desimone R, Gross CG (1981) Visual properties of neurons in a polysensory area in superior temporal sulcus of the macaque. J Neurophysiol 46: 369–384.

Buccino G, Vogt S, Ritzl A, Fink GR, Zilles K, Freund HJ, Rizzolatti G (2004) Neural circuits underlying imitation of hand actions: an event related fMRI study. Neuron 42: 323–34.

Colapietro V., (1988), "Human Agency: The Habits of Our Being."

Southern Journal of Philosophy, XXVI, 2, pp. 153-68.

Colapietro V., (1992), "Purpose, Power, and Agency." The Monist, 75, 4 (October) pp. 423-44.

Colapietro V., (2003), "Signs and their vicissitudes: Meanings in excess of consciousness and functionality." Logica, Dialogica, Ideologica, a cure di Susan Petrilli e Patrizia Calefato (Milano: Mimesis), pp. 221-36.

Colapietro V., (2004a), "C. S. Peirce's Reclamation of Teleology." Nature in American Philosophy, ed. Jean De Groot (Washington, D.C.: Catholic University Press of America), pp. 88-108.

Colapietro V., (2004b), "Portrait of a Historicist: An Alternative Reading of Peircean Semiotic." Semiotiche, 2/04 [maggio 2004], pp. 49-68.

Colapietro V., (2006), "Engaged Pluralism: Between Alterity and

Sociality." The Pragmatic Century: Conversations with Richard J. Bernstein (Albany, NY: SUNY Press), pp. 39-68.

Colapietro V., (2009), "Habit, Competence, and Purpose." Forthcoming in The Transactions of the Charles S. Peirce Society.

Calder AJ, Keane J, Manes F, Antoun N, Young AW (2000) Impaired recognition and experience of disgust following brain injury. Nature Neurosci 3: 1077–1078.

Carey DP, Perrett DI, Oram MW (1997) Recognizing, understanding and reproducing actions. In: Jeannerod M, Grafman J (eds) Handbook of neuropsychology. Vol. 11: Action and cognition. Elsevier, Amsterdam.

Carr L, Iacoboni M, Dubeau MC, Mazziotta JC, Lenzi GL (2003) Neural mechanisms of empathy in humans: a relay from neural systems for imitation to limbic areas. Proc Natl Acad Sci USA 100: 5497–5502.

Changeux JP, Ricoeur P (1998) La nature et la règle. Odile Jacob, Paris.

Cochin S, Barthelemy C, Roux S, Martineau J (1999) Observation and execution of movement: similarities demonstrated by quantified electroencephalograpy. Eur J Neurosci 11: 1839– 1842.

Chomsky Noam, (2017) Requiem for the American Dream

Chomsky Noam, (2016) Who Rules the World?

Chomsky Noam, (2010) How the World Works

Churchland, P.S. (1986), Neurophilosophy (Cambridge, MA: The MIT Press).

Churchland, P.S. & Ramachandran, V.S. (1993), 'Filling in: Why Dennett is wrong', in Dennett and His Critics: Demystifying Mind, ed. B. Dahlbom (Oxford: Blackwell Scientific Press).

Churchland, P.S., Ramachandran, V.S. & Sejnowski, T.J. (1994), 'A critique of pure vision', in Large- scale Neuronal Theories of the Brain, ed. C. Koch & J.L. Davis (Cambridge, MA: The MIT Press).

Crick, F. (1994), The Astonishing Hypothesis: The Scientific Search for the Soul (New York: Simon and Schuster).

Crick, F. (1996), 'Visual perception: rivalry and consciousness', Nature, 379.

Crick, F. & Koch, C. (1992), 'The problem of consciousness', Scientific American, 267.

Craig AD (2002) How do you feel? Interoception: the sense of the physiological condition of the body. Nature Rev Neurosci 3: 655–666.

Damasio, A (2003a) Looking for Spinoza. Harcourt Inc. Damasio A (2003b) Feeling of emotion and the self. Ann NY Acad Sci 1001: 253–261.

d'Aquili, Eugene. "Senses of Reality in Science and Religion." Zygon 17, no 4 (1982)

d'Aquili, Eugene. "The Biopsychological Determinants of Religious Ritual Behavior." Zygon 10, no. 1 (1975)

d'Aquili, Eugene. "The Myth-Ritual Complex: A Biogenetic Structural Analysis." Zygon 18, no. 3 (1983)

d'Aquili, Eugene, and Andrew Newberg. The Mystical Mind: Probing the Biology of Religious Experience. Minneapolis: Fortress Press, 1999.

Daly DD. 1958. Ictal affect. Am J Psychiatry.

Damasio, A. (1994) Descartes' Error: Emotion, Reason and the Human Brain. New York, Putnams.

Damasio, A. (1999) The Feeling of What Happens: Body, Emotion and the Making of Consciousness. London, Heinemann.

Darwin, C. (1859) On the Origin of Species by Means of Natural Selection. London, Murray.

Darwin, C. (1871) The Descent of Man and Selection in Relation to Sex. London, John Murray.

Darwin, C. (1872) The Expression of the Emotions in Man and Animals. London, John Murray; also published 1965, Chicago, University of Chicago Press.

Dawkins, M.S. (1987) Minding and mattering. In C. Blakemore and S. Greenfield (eds) Mindwaves. Oxford, Blackwell, 151-60.

Dawkins, R. (1976) The Selfish Gene. Oxford, Oxford University Press; a new edition, with additional material, was published in 1989.

Dawkins, R. (1986) The Blind Watchmaker. London, Longman.

Di Pellegrino G, Fadiga L, Fogassi L, Gallese V, Rizzolatti G (1992) Understanding motor events: A neurophysiological study. Exp Brain Res 91: 176–80.

Deikman, A.J. (2000) A functional approach to mysticism. Journal of Consciousness Studies 7(11-12), 75-91.

Delmonte, M.M. (1987) Personality and meditation. In M. West (ed.) The Psychology of Meditation. Oxford, Clarendon Press, 118-32.

Dennett, D.C. (1987) The Intentional Stance. Cambridge, MA, MIT Press.

Dennett, D.C. (1988) Quining qualia. In A.J. Marcel and E. Bisiach (eds)

Consciousness in Contemporary Science. Oxford, Oxford University Press, 42-77.

Dennett, D.C. (1991) Consciousness Explained. Boston, MA, and London, Little, Brown and Co.

Dennett, D.C. (1995a) Darwin's Dangerous Idea. London, Penguin.

Dennett, D.C. (1995b) The unimagined preposterousness of zombies. Journal of Consciousness Studies 2(4), 322-6.

Dennett, D.C. (1995c) Cog: steps towards consciousness in robots. In T. Metzinger (ed.) Conscious Experience. Thorverton, Devon, Imprint Academic, 471-87.

Dennett, D.C. (1995d) The path not taken. Behavioral and Brain Sciences 18, 252-3; commentary on N. Block, On a confusion about a function of consciousness. Behavioral and Brain Sciences 18, 227.

Dennett, D.C. (1996a) Facing backwards on the problem of consciousness. Journal of Consciousness Studies 3(1), 4-6.

Dennett, D.C. (1996b) Kinds of Minds: Towards an Understanding of Consciousness. London, Weidenfeld & Nicolson.

Dennett, D.C. (1997) An exchange with Daniel Dennett. In J. Searle (ed.) The Mystery of Consciousness. New York, New York Review of Books, 115-19.

Dennett, D.C. (1998) The myth of double transduction. In S.R. Hameroff, A.W. Kaszniak and A. C. Scott (eds) Toward a Science of Consciousness: The Second Tucson Discussions and Debates. Cambridge, MA, MIT Press, 97-107.

Dennett, D.C. (1998b) Brainchildren: Essays on Designing Minds. Cambridge, MA, MIT Press.

Dennett, D.C. (2001) The fantasy of first person science. Debate with D. Chalmers, Northwestern University, Evanston, IL, February 2001.

Dennett, D.C. (2003) Freedom Evolves. New York, Penguin.

Dennett, D.C. and Kinsbourne, M. (1992) Time and the observer: the where and when of consciousness in the brain. Behavioral and Brain Sciences 15, 183-247, including commentaries and authors' responses.

Dewey J., (1911 [1977]), "Epistemological Realism: The Alleged Ubiquity of the Knowledge Relation." Journal of Philosophy, VIII, 20 (September 28, 1911).

Dewhurst, Kenneth, and A. W. Beard. "Sudden Religious Conversions in Temporal Lobe Epilepsy." British Journal of Psychiatry 117 (1970)

Dewhurst K, Beard AW. Sudden religious conversions in temporal lobe epilepsy. 1970 Epilepsy Behav 2003

Devinsky O, Lai G. Spirituality and religion in epilepsy. Epilepsy Behav 2008.

Devinsky, O., Morrell, MJ, Vogt, BA. (1995) 'Contribution of anterior cingulate cortex to behavior', Brain, 118.

E. Horvitz, "One Hundred Year Study on Artificial Intelligence: Reflections and Framing," ed: Stanford University, 2014.

Eckhart Meister, Selected Writings

Egidi R., ed. (1999), "Von Wright and 'Dante's Dream': Stages in a Philosophical Pilgrim's Progress", in In Search of a New Humanism: the Philosophy of G.H. von Wright, ed. by R. Egidi, Kluwer, Dordrecht.

Fadiga L, Fogassi L, Pavesi G, Rizzolatti G (1995) Motor facilitation during action observation: a magnetic stimulation study. J Neurophysiol 73: 2608–2611.

Fogassi L, Gallese V, Fadiga L, Rizzolatti G (1998) Neurons responding to the sight of goal directed hand/arm actions in the parietal area PF (7b) of the macaque monkey. Soc Neurosci Abs 24:257.5.

Frith U, Frith CD (2003) Development and neurophysiology of mentalizing. Philos Trans R Soc Lond B Biol Sci 358: 459.

Farah, M.J. (1989), 'The neural basis of mental imagery', Trends in Neurosciences, 10.

Finlay BL, Darlington RB (1995) Linked regularities in the development and evolution of mammalian brains. Science 268.

Freud, S. "The Interpretation of Dreams", 1900

Freud, S. "Selected papers on hysteria and other psychoneuroses" Journal of Nervous and Mental Disease 1909.

Freud, S. "The Origin and Development of Psychoanalysis", 1910

Freud, S. "Psychopathology of everyday life", 1914

Freud, S. "Beyond the Pleasure Principle", 1920

Frith, C.D. & Dolan, R.J. (1997), 'Abnormal beliefs: Delusions and memory', Paper presented at the May, 1997, Harvard Conference on Memory and Belief.

Gay, Volney, ed. Neuroscience and Religion. Plymouth, UK: Lexington Books, 2009.

Gazzaniga, M. S. (1985). The social brain. New York: Basic Books.

Gazzaniga, M.S. (1993), 'Brain mechanisms and conscious experience', Ciba Foundation Symposium, 174.

Geschwind N. "Behavioural changes in temporal lobe epilepsy". Psychol Med. 1979.

Gellhorn, E., Kiely, W.F. "Mystical states of consciousness: neurophysiological and clinical aspects." J Nerv Ment Dis. 1972;154:399-405.

Gilbert SL, Dobyns WB, Lahn BT (2005) Genetic links between brain development and brain evolution. Nat Rev Genet 6.

Gray JA. The Psychology of Fear and Stress. 2nd ed. New York, NY: Cambridge University Press; 1988.

Gloor, P. (1992), 'Amygdala and temporal lobe epilepsy', in The Amygdala: Neurobiological Aspects of Emotion, Memory and Mental

Dysfunction, ed J.P. Aggleton (New York: Wiley-Liss).

Greenspan, S. I. and S. G. Shanker (2004). The first idea: How symbols, language, and intelligence evolved from our early primate ancestors to modern humans. Cambridge, MA: Da Capo Press.

Grady, D. (1993), 'The vision thing: Mainly in the brain', Discover, June.

Gallagher HL, Frith CD (2003) Functional imaging of 'theory of mind'. Trends Cogn Sci 7: 77.

Gallese V, Fogassi L, Fadiga L, Rizzolatti G (2002) Action representation and the inferior parietal lobule. In: Prinz W, Hommel B (eds) Attention & Performance XIX. Common mechanisms in perception and action. Oxford University Press, Oxford.

Gallese V, Keysers C, Rizzolatti G (2004) A unifying view of the basis of social cognition. Trends Cogn Sci 8: 396–403.

Gangitano M, Mottaghy FM, Pascual-Leone A (2001) Phase specific modulation of cortical motor output during movement observation. NeuroReport 12: 1489–1492.

Gangitano M, Mottaghy FM, Pascual-Leone A (2004) Modulation of premotor mirror neuron activity during observation of unpredictable grasping movements. Eur J Neurosci 20: 2193– 2202.

Goldman AI, Sripada CS (2004) Simulationist models of face-based emotion recognition. Cognition 94: 193–213.

Grèzes J, Costes N, Decety J (1998) Top-down effect of strategy on the perception of human biological motion: a PET investigation. Cogn Neuropsychol 15: 553–582.

Grèzes J, Armony JL, Rowe J, Passingham RE (2003) Activations related to "mirror" and "canonical" neurones in the human brain: an fMRI study. Neuroimage 18: 928–937.

Gross CG, Rocha-Miranda CE, Bender DB (1972) Visual properties of neurons in the inferotemporal cortex of the macaque. J Neurophysiol 35: 96–111.

Hari R, Forss N, Avikainen S, Kirveskari S, Salenius S, Rizzolatti G (1998) Activation of human primary motor cortex during action observation: a neuromagnetic study. Proc. Natl Acad Sci USA 95: 15061–15065.

Hall, Daniel, Keith Meador, and Harold Koenig. "Measuring Religiousness in Health Research: Review and Critique." Journal of Religion and Health 47, no. 2 (2008)

Harris, Sam, Jonas Kaplan, Ashley Curiel, Susan Bookheimer, Marco

Iacoboni, and Mark Cohen. "The Neural Correlates of Religious and Nonreligious Belief." PLoS One 4, no. 10 (October 1, 2009)

Halgren, E. (1992), 'Emotional neurophysiology of the amygdala within the context of human cognition', in The Amygdala: Neurobiological Aspects of Emotion, Memory and Mental Dysfunction, ed J.P. Aggleton (New York: Wiley-Liss).

Halligan PW, Fink GR, Marshal JC, Vallar G. 2003. Spatial cognition: evidence from visual neglect. Trends Cogn Sci.

Handbook of Emotions, Edited by Michael Lewis, Jeannette M. Haviland-Jones, and Lisa Feldman Barrett, The Guilford Press; 3rd edition (2010).

Haggard, P., Clark, S. and Kalogeras,]. (2002) Voluntary action and conscious awareness, Nature Neuroscience 5, 382-5. Haggard, P., Newman, C. and

Magno, E. (1999) On the perceived time of voluntary actions. British Journal of Psychology 90, 291-303.

Hameroff, S.R. and Penrose, R. (1996) Conscious events as orchestrated space-time selections. Journal of Consciousness Studies 3(1), 36-53; also reprinted in J. Shear (ed.) (1997) Explaining Consciousness-The Hard Problem. Cambridge, MA, MIT Press, 177-95.

Hardcastle, V.G. (2000) How to understand theN in NCC. InT. Metzinger (ed.) Neural Correlates of Consciousness. Cambridge, MA, MIT Press, 259-64.

Harding, D.E. (1961) On Having no Head: Zen and the Re-Discovery of the Obvious. London, Buddhist Society.

Hardy, A. (1979) The Spiritual Nature of Man: A Study of Contemporary Religious Experience. Oxford, Clarendon Press.

Hamad, S. (1990) The symbol grounding problem. Physica D 42, 335-46.

Hamad, S. (2001) No easy way out. The Sciences 41(2), 36-42.

Harre, R. and Gillett, G. (1994) The Discursive Mind. Thousand Oaks, CA, Sage.

Haugeland, J. (ed.) (1997) Mind Design II: Philosophy, Psychology, Artificial Intelligence. Cambridge, MA, MIT Press.

Hauser, M.D. (2000) Wild Minds: What Animals Really Think. New York, Henry Holt and Co.; London, Penguin.

Hearne, K. (1990) The Dream Machine. Northants, Aquarian.

Hebb, D.O. (1949) The Organization of Behavior. New York, Wiley.

Helmholtz, H.L.F. von (1856-67) Treatise on Physiological Optics.

Heyes, C.M. (1998) Theory of mind in nonhuman primates. Behavioral and Brain Sciences 21, 101-48; with commentaries.

Heyes, C.M. and Galef, B.G. (eds) (1996) Social Learning in Animals: The Roots of Culture. San Diego, CA, Academic Press.

Hilgard, E.R. (1986) Divided Consciousness: Multiple Controls in Human Thought and Action. New York, Wiley.

Hocquette JF (2016) Is in vitro meat the

solution for the future? Meat Science 120:

167–176

Hodgson, R. (1891) A case of double consciousness. Proceedings of the Society for Psychical Research 7, 221-58.

Hofstadter, D.R. (1979) Code!, Escher, Bach: An Eternal Golden Braid. London, Penguin.

Hofstadter, D.R. and Dennett, D.C. (eds) (1981) The Mind's I: Fantasies and Reflections on Self and Soul. London, Penguin.

Holland, J. (ed.) (2001) Ecstasy: The Complete Guide: A Comprehensive Look at the Risks and Benefits of MDMA. Rochester, VT, Park Street Press.

Holmes, D.S. (1987) The influence of meditation versus rest on physiological arousal. In M. West (ed.) The Psychology of Meditation. Oxford, Clarendon Press, 81-103.

Holt, J. (1999) Blindsight in debates about qualia. Journal of Consciousness Studies 6(5), 54-71.

Horgan, J. (1994), 'Can science explain consciousness?', Scientific American, 271.

Holloway RL (1996) Evolution of the human brain. In: Lock A, Peters CR (eds) Handbook of human symbolic evolution. Oxford University Press, Oxford

Iacoboni M, Woods RP, Brass M, Bekkering H, Mazziotta JC, Rizzolatti G (1999) Cortical mechanisms of human imitation. Science 286: 2526–2528.

Iacoboni M, Koski LM, Brass M, Bekkering H, Woods RP, Dubeau MC, Mazziotta JC, Rizzolatti G (2001) Reafferent copies of imitated actions in the right superior temporal cortex. Proc Natl Acad Sci USA 98: 13995–13999.

Jeannerod M (1988) The neural and behavioural organization of goal-directed movements. Clarendon Press, Oxford.

Johnson-Frey SH, Maloof FR, Newman-Norlund R, Farrer C, Inati S,

Grafton ST (2003) Actions or hand-objects interactions? Human inferior frontal cortex and action observation. Neuron 39: 1053–1058.

Jackson, F. (1982) Epiphenomenal qualia. Philosophical Quarterly 32, 127-36.

James, W. (1890) The Principles of Psychology (2 volumes). London, Macmillan.

James, W. (1902) The Varieties of Religious Experience: A Study in Human Nature. New York and London, Longmans, Green and Co.

Jansen, K. (2001) Ketamine: Dreams and Realities. Sarasota, FL, Multidisciplinary Association for Psychedelic Studies.

Jay, M. (ed.) (1999) Artificial Paradises: A Drugs Reader. London, Penguin.

Jaynes, J. (1976) The Origin of Consciousness in the Breakdown of the Bicameral Mind. New York, Houghton Mifflin.

Johnson, M.K. and Raye, C.L. (1981) Reality monitoring. Psychological Review 88, 67-85.

Kadim I, Mahgoub O, Baqir S et al. (2015) Cultured meat from muscle stem cells: a review of challenges and prospects. J Integr Agr 14: 222–233

Koski L, Iacoboni M, Dubeau MC, Woods RP, Mazziotta JC (2003) Modulation of cortical activity during different imitative behaviors. J Neurophysiol 89: 460–471.

Krolak-Salmon P, Henaff MA, Isnard J, Tallon-Baudry C, Guenot M, Vighetto A, Bertrand O, Mauguiere F (2003) An attention modulated response to disgust in human ventral anterior insula. Ann Neurol 53: 446–453.

Kandel, E. R. In Search of Memory: The Emergence of a New Science of

Mind, W. W. Norton & Company (2007).

Kandel E. R. Schwartz JH, Jessel TM. Principles of neural sciences. New York; McGraw Hill, 2000.

Kanizsa, G. (1979), Organization In Vision (New York: Praeger).

Kaloupek DG, Scott JR, Khatami V. Assessment of coping strategies associated with syncope in blood donors. J Psychosom Res. 1985;29:207-214.

Kanwisher, N. (2001) Neural events and perceptual awareness. Cognition 79, 89-113; also reprinted inS. Dehaene (ed.) The Cognitive Neuroscience of Consciousness. Cambridge, MA, MIT Press, 89-113.

Kapleau, Roshi P. (1980) The Three Pillars of Zen: Teaching, Practice, and Enlightenment (revised edn). New York, Doubleday.

Karn, K. and Hayhoe, M. (2000) Memory representations guide targeting eye movements in a natural task. Visual Cognition 7, 673-703.

Kasamatsu, A. and Hirai, T. (1966) An electroencephalographic study on the Zen meditation (zazen). Folia Psychiatrica et Neurologica Japonica 20, 315-36.

Kaiserman-Abramof, I. R., Graybiel, A. M., & Nauta, W. J. (1980). The thalamic projection to cortical area 17 in a congenitally anophthalmic mouse strain. Neuroscience, 5, 41–52.

Kanold, P. O., Kara, P., Reid, R. C., & Shatz, C. J. (2003). Role of subplate neurons in functional maturation of visual cortical columns. Science, 301, 521–525.

Kennedy, H., & Dehay, C. (1988). Functional implications of the anatomical organization of the callosal projections of visual areas V1 and V2 in the macaque monkey. Behav. Brain Res., 29, 225–236.

Kennedy, H., & Dehay, C. (1993). Cortical specifi cation of mice and men. Cereb. Cortex, 3, 171–186.

Kentridge, R.W. and Heywood, C.A. (1999) The status of blindsight. Journal of Consciousness Studies 6(5), 3-11.

Kihlstrom, J.F. (1996) Perception without awareness of what is perceived, learning without awareness of what is learned. In M. Velmans (ed.) The Science of Consciousness. London, Routledge, 23-46.

Kluver, H. (1926) Mescal visions and eidetic vision. American Journal of Psychology 37, 502-15.

Kollerstrom, N. (1999) The path of Halley's comet, and Newton's late apprehension of the law of gravity. Annals of Science 56, 331-56.

Kosslyn, S.M. (1980) Image and Mind. Cambridge, MA, Harvard University Press.

Kosslyn, S.M. (1988) Aspects of a cognitive neuroscience of mental imagery. Science 240, 1621-6.

Kinsbourne, M. (1995), 'The intralaminar thalamic nucleii', Consciousness and Cognition, 4.

Kjaer, Troels, Camilla Bertelsen, Paola Piccini, David Brooks, Jorgen Alving, and Hans Lou. "Increased Dopamine Tone during Meditation- Induced Change of Consciousness." Cognitive Brain Research 13, no. 2 (April 2002)

Kölmel HW. 1985. Complex visual hallucinations in the hemianopic field. J Neurol Neurosurg Psychiatry.

Koenig, Harold. "Research on Religion, Spirituality, and Mental Health: A Review." Canadian Journal of Psychiatry 54, no. 5 (May 2009)

Koenig, Harold, ed. Handbook of Religion and Mental Health. San Diego, CA: Academic Press, 1998

Kraepelin E. Psychiatry: A Textbook for Students and Physicians. New York, NY: Science History Publications; 1990.

Lauglin, Charles, John McManus, and Eugene d'Aquili. Brain, Symbol, and Experience. 2nd ed. New York: Columbia University Press, 1992

Lakoff, G. and M. Johnson (1999). Philosophy in the flesh. Basic Books: New York.

LeDoux, J. E. (1996). The emotional brain. New York: Simon & Schuster.

LeDoux, J.E. (1992), 'Emotion and the amygdala', in The Amygdala: Neurobiological Aspects of Emo- tion, Memory and Mental Dysfunction, ed J.P. Aggleton (New York: Wiley-Liss).

Levin, D.T. and Simons, D.J. (1997) Failure to detect changes to attended objects in motion pictures. Psychonomic Bulletin and Review 4, 501-6.

Levine,J. (1983) Materialism and qualia: the explanatory gap. Pacific Philosophical Quarterly 64, 354-61.

Levine,J. (2001) Purple Haze: The Puzzle of Consciousness. New York, Oxford University Press. Levine, S. (1979) A Gradual Awakening. New York, Doubleday.

Levinson, B.W. (1965) States of awareness during general anaesthesia. British Journal of Anaesthesia 37, 544-6.

Lewicki, P., Czyzewska, M. and Hoffman, H. (1987) Unconscious acquisition of complex procedural knowledge. Journal of Experimental Psychology: Learning, Memory and Cognition 13, 523-30.

Lewicki, P., Hill, T. and Bizot, E. (1988) Acquisition of procedural knowledge about a pattern of stimuli that cannot be articulated. Cognitive Psychology 20, 24-37.

Lewicki, P., Hill, T. and Czyzewska, M. (1992) Nonconscious acquisition of information. American Psychologist 47, 796-801.

Manthey S, Schubotz RI, von Cramon DY (2003). Premotor cortex in observing erroneous action: an fMRI study. Brain Res Cogn Brain Res 15: 296–307.

M. Colombo, "Why build a virtual brain? Large-scale neural simulations as jump start for cognitive computing," Journal of Experimental and Theoretical Artificial Intelligence, vol. 29, pp. 361-370, 2017.

Mesulam MM, Mufson EJ (1982) Insula of the old world monkey. III: Efferent cortical output and comments on function. J Comp Neurol 212: 38–52.

Naskar, Abhijit. "What is Mind?", 2016

Naskar, Abhijit. "In Search of Divinity: Journey to The Kingdom of Conscience", 2016

Naskar, Abhijit. "Love, God & Neurons: Memoir of A Scientist who found himself by getting lost", 2016

Naskar, Abhijit. "Neurons of Jesus: Mind of A Teacher, Spouse & Thinker", 2017

Naskar, Abhijit. "Rowdy Buddha: The First Sapiens", 2017

Naskar, Abhijit. "The Education Decree", 2017

Naskar, Abhijit. "Principia Humanitas", 2017

Naskar, Abhijit. "We Are All Black: A Treatise on Racism", 2017

Naskar, Abhijit. "Wise Mating: A Treatise on Monogamy", 2017

Naskar, Abhijit. "Illusion of Religion: A Treatise on Religious Fundamentalism", 2017

Naskar, Abhijit. "I Am The Thread: My Mission", 2017

Naskar, Abhijit. "Morality Absolute", 2017

Naskar, Abhijit. "Fabric of Humanity", 2018

Naskar, Abhijit. "The Constitution of The United Peoples of Earth", 2019

Naskar, Abhijit. "When Humans Unite: Making A World Without Borders", 2019

Naskar, Abhijit. "Mission Reality", 2019

Naskar, Abhijit. "Citizens of Peace: Beyond The Savagery of Sovereignty", 2019

Naskar, Abhijit. "Neurons Giveth, Neurons Taketh Away | Abhijit

Naskar | TEDxIIMRanchi", 2019 https://www.youtube.com/watch?v=B NX-Q0ySm80

Newberg, Andrew, and Jeremy Iversen. "The Neural Basis of the Complex Mental Task of Meditation: Neurotransmitter and Neurochemical Considerations." Medical Hypotheses 61, no. 2 (2003).

Newberg, Andrew. "How God Changes Your Brain: An Introduction to Jewish Neurotheology", CCAR Journal: The Reform Jewish Quarterly, Winter 2016.

Newberg, Andrew, and Stephanie Newberg. "A Neuropsychological Perspective on Spiritual Development." In Handbook of Spiritual Development in Childhood and Adolescence, edited by Eugene Roehlkepartain, Pamela King, Linda Wagener, and Peter Benson. London: Sage Publications, Inc., 2005

Newberg, Andrew. "The Neurotheology Link An Intersection Between Spirituality and Health", Alternative and Complimentary Therapies, Vol 21 No 1, February 2015.

Newberg, Andrew, Nancy Wintering, Dharma Khalsa, Hannah Roggenkamp, and Mark Waldman. "Meditation Effects on Cognitive Function and Cerebral Blood Flow in Subjects with Memory Loss: A Preliminary Study." Journal of Alzheimer's Disease 20, no. 2 (2010)

Nash, M. (1995), 'Glimpses of the mind', Time.

Nesse RM. Proximate and evolutionary studies of anxiety, stress and depression: synergy at the interface. Neurosci Biobehav Rev. 1999;23:895-903.

Nishitani N, Hari R (2000) Temporal dynamics of cortical representation for action. Proc Natl Acad Sci USA 97: 913–918.

Nishitani N, Hari R (2002) Viewing lip forms: cortical dynamics. Neuron 36: 1211–1220.

O'Hara, K. and Scutt, T. (1996) There is no hard problem of consciousness. Journal of Consciousness Studies 3(4), 290-302, reprinted in J. Shear (ed.) (1997) Explaining Consciousness. Cambridge, MA, MIT Press, 69-82.

O'Regan, J.K. (1992) Solving the "real" mysteries of visual perception: the world as an outside memory. Canadian Journal of Psychology 46, 461-88.

O'Regan, J.K. and Noe, A. (2001) A sensorimotor account of vision and visual consciousness. Behavioral and Brain Sciences 24(5), 883-917.

O'Regan, J.K., Rensink, R.A. and Clark,].]. (1999) Change-blindness as a result of "mudsplashes." Nature 398, 34.

Ornstein, R.E. (1977) The Psychology of Consciousness (2nd edn). New York, Harcourt.

Ornstein, R.E. (1986) The Psychology of Consciousness (3rd edn). New York, Pehguin.

Ornstein, R.E. (1992) The Evolution of Consciousness. New York, Touchstone.

Penfield W, Faulk ME (1955) The insula: further observations on its function. Brain 78: 445– 470.

Penrose, R. (1994), Shadows of the Mind (Oxford: Oxford University Press).

Penrose, R. (1989), The Emperor's New Mind: Concerning Computers, Minds and The Laws of Physics (Oxford: Oxford University Press).

Persinger, "'I would kill in God's name' role of sex, weekly church attendance, report of a religious experience and limbic lability" Perceptual and Motor Skills 1997.

Persinger "Experimental simulation of the God experience" Neurotheology 2003.

Persinger, M. A. (1993b). Personality changes following brain injury as a grief response to the loss of sense of self: Phenomenological themes as indices of local lability and neurocognitive restructuring as psycho- therapy. Psychological Reports, 72

Persinger, Corradini, Clement, Keaney, et al "Neurotheology and its convergence with neuroquantology" NeuroQuantology 2010.

Persinger, Koren and St-Pierre "The electromagnetic induction of mystical and altered states within the laboratory" Journal of Consciousness Exploration and Research 2010.

Persinger "Case report: A prototypical spontaneous 'sensed presence' of a sentient being and concomitant electroencephalographic activity in the clinical laboratory" Neurocase 2008.

Persinger and Saroka "Potential production of Hughlings Jackson's "parasitic consciousness" by physiologically-patterned weak transcerebral magnetic fields: QEEG and source localization" Epilepsy & Behavior 28 (2013).

Persinger. "The neuropsychiatry of paranormal experiences". J Neuropsychiatry Clin Neurosci 2001.

Persinger. "Neuropsychological bases of god beliefs", New York: Praeger, 1987

Persinger. "Temporal lobe epileptic signs and correlative behaviors displayed by normal populations", Journal of General Psychology, 1986

Persinger "Experimental Facilitation of the Sensed Presence: Possible Intercalation between the Hemispheres Induced by Complex Magnetic Fields" Journal of Nervous and Mental Disease 2002.

Palmer J. 1978. The out-of-body experience: a psychological theory. Parapsychol Rev.

Page AC. Blood-injury phobia. Clinical Psychology Review. 1994;14:443-461.

Perry BD, Pollard R. Homeostasis, stress, trauma, and adaptation. A neurodevelopmental view of childhood trauma. Child Adolesc Psychiatr Clin N Am. 1998;7:33.

Paré, D. & Llinás, R. (1995), 'Conscious and preconscious processes as seen from the standpoint of sleep-waking cycle neurophysiology', Neuropsychologia, 33.

P. S. de Laplace. Essai Philosophique sur les Probabilites [1814], in Academy des Sciences, Oeuvres Complotes de Laplace, Vol. 7, Gauthier-Villars, Paris (1886).

Perrett DI, Harries MH, Bevan R, Thomas S, Benson PJ, Mistlin AJ, Chitty AJ, Hietanen JK, Ortega JE (1989) Frameworks of analysis for the neural representation of animate objects and actions. J Exp Bio 146: 87–113.

Phillips ML, Young AW, Senior C, Brammer M, Andrew C, Calder AJ, Bullmore ET, Perrett DI, Rowland D, Williams SC, Gray JA, David AS (1997) A specific neural substrate for perceiving facial expressions of disgust. Nature 389: 495–498.

Phillips ML, Young AW, Scott SK, Calder AJ, Andrew C, Giampietro V, Williams SC, Bullmore ET, Brammer M, Gray JA (1998) Neural responses to facial and vocal expressions of fear and disgust. Proc R Soc Lond B Biol Sci 265: 1809–1817.

Puce A, Perrett D (2003) Electrophysiological and brain imaging of biological motion. Philosoph Trans Royal Soc Lond, Series B, 358: 435–445.

Ramachandran VS. Behavioral and magnetoencephalographic correlates of plasticity in the adult human brain. Proc Natl Acad Sci USA 1993; 90: 10413–20.

Ramachandran VS. Phantom limbs, neglect syndromes, repressed memories, and Freudian psychology. Int Rev Neurobiol 1994; 37: 291–333.

Ramachandran VS. Plasticity and functional recovery in neurology. Clin Med 2005; 5: 368–73.

Ramachandran VS, Hirstein W. The perception of phantom limbs. The D. O. Hebb lecture. Brain 1998; 121: 1603–30.

Ramachandran VS, McGeoch PD, Williams L, Arcilla G. Rapid relief of thalamic pain syndrome induced by vestibular caloric stimulation. Neurocase 2007; 13: 185–8.

Ramachandran VS, Rogers-Ramachandran D, Cobb S. Touching the phantom limb. Nature 1995; 377: 489–90.

Ramachandran VS, Rogers-Ramachandran D. Phantom limbs and neural plasticity. Arch Neurol 2000; 57: 317–20.

Ramachandran VS, Rogers-Ramachandran D. It's all done with mirrors. Sci Am Mind 2007; 18: 16–9.

Ramachandran VS, Rogers-Ramachandran D. Sensations referred to a patient's phantom arm from another subjects intact arm: perceptual correlates of mirror neurons. Med Hypotheses 2008; 70: 1233–4.

Ramachandran VS, Rogers-Ramachandran D, Stewart M. Perceptual correlates of massive cortical reorganization. Science 1992; 258: 1159–60.

Rizzolatti G, Craighero L (2004) The mirror-neuron system. Annu Rev Neurosci 27: 169–192.

Rizzolatti G, Scandolara C, Matelli M, Gentilucci M (1981) Afferent properties of periarcuate neurons in macaque monkeys. I. Somatosensory responses. Behav Brain Res 2: 125–146.

Rizzolatti G, Fadiga L, Matelli M, Bettinardi V, Paulesu E, Perani D, Fazio F (1996) Localization of grasp representation in humans by PET: 1. Observation versus execution. Exp Brain Res 111: 246–252.

Rizzolatti G, Fogassi L, Gallese V (2001) Neurophysiological mechanisms underlying the understanding and imitation of action. Nature Rev Neurosci 2:661–670.

Rock I, Victor J. Vision and touch: an experimentally created conflict between the two senses. Science 1964; 143: 594–6.

Rose´n B, Lundborg G. Training with a mirror in rehabilitation of the hand. Scand J Plast Reconstr Surg Hand Surg 2005; 39: 104–8.

Royet JP, Plailly J, Delon-Martin C, Kareken DA, Segebarth C (2003) fMRI of emotional responses to odors: influence of hedonic valence and judgment, handedness, and gender. Neuroimage 20: 713–728.

Rozin R Haidt J and McCauley CR (2000) Disgust. In: Lewis M, Haviland-Jones JM (eds) Handbook of Emotion. 2nd Edition. Guilford Press, New York, pp 637–653.

Saxe R, Carey S, Kanwisher N (2004) Understanding other minds: linking developmental psychology and functional neuroimaging. Annu Rev Psychol 55: 87–124.

S. J. Russell and P. Norvig, Artificial intelligence: a modern approach (3rd edition): Prentice Hall, 2009.

Schienle A, Stark R, Walter B, Blecker C, Ott U, Kirsch P, Sammer G, Vaitl D (2002) The insula is not specifically involved in disgust processing: an fMRI study. Neuroreport 13: 2023–2026.

Showers MJC, Lauer EW (1961) Somatovisceral motor patterns in the insula. J Comp Neurol 117: 107–115.

Singer T, Seymour B, O'Doherty J, Kaube H, Dolan RJ, Frith CD (2004) Empathy for pain involves the affective but not the sensory components of pain. Science 303: 1157–1162.

Small DM, Gregory MD, Mak YE, Gitelman D, Mesulam MM, Parrish T

(2003) Dissociation of neural representation of intensity and affective valuation in human gustation Neuron 39: 701–711.

Smith A (1759) The theory of moral sentiments (ed. 1976). Clarendon Press, Oxford.

Sprengelmeyer R, Rausch M, Eysel UT, Przuntek H (1998) Neural structures associated with recognition of facial expressions of basic emotions Proc R Soc Lond B Biol Sci 265: 1927–1931.

Strafella AP, Paus T (2000) Modulation of cortical excitability during action observation: a transcranial magnetic stimulation study. NeuroReport 11: 2289–2292.

Simonsen R (2015) Eating for the future: veganism and the challenge of in vitro meat. In: Stapleton P, Byers A (Hg). Biopolitics and utopia. Palgrave Macmillan, New York (2015), S 167–190

Tanaka K (1996) Inferotemporal cortex and object vision. Ann Rev Neurosci. 19: 109–140.

T. R. Society, "Machine learning: the power and promise of computers that learn by example," ed. The Royal Society, 2017.

Tomasello M, Call J (1997) Primate cognition. Oxford University Press, Oxford.

Tremblay C, Robert M, Pascual-Leone A, Lepore F, Nguyen DK, Carmant L, Bouthillier A, Theoret H (2004) Action observation and execution: intracranial recordings in a human subject. Neurology. 63: 937–938.

Umilta MA, Kohler E, Gallese V, Fogassi L, Fadiga L, Keysers C, Rizzolatti G (2001) "I know what you are doing": a neurophysiological study. Neuron 32: 91–101.

Von Wright G.H., (1963), Norm and Action. A Logical Inquiry, Routledge & Kegan Paul, London.

Von Wright G.H., (1976), "Determinism and the Study of Man", in Essays on Explanation and Understanding, ed. by J. Manninen and R. Tuomela, Reidel, Dordrecht.

Von Wright G.H., (1977), "What is Humanism?", The Lindlay Lecture, University of Arkansas, Lawrence, Kansas.

Von Wright G.H., (1979), "Humanism and the Humanities", in Philosophy and Grammar, ed. by S. Kanger and S. Öhman, Reidel, Dordrecht, pp. 1-16. Reprinted in von Wright (1993).

Von Wright G.H., (1980), Freedom and Determination, North-Holland Publishing Co., Amsterdam.

Von Wright G.H., (1985), Of Human Freedom, The Tanner Lectures on Human Values,

Vol. VI, ed. by S. M. McMurrin, University of Utah Press, Salt Lake City, pp. 107-70. Reprinted in von Wright (1998).

Von Wright G.H., (1993), The Tree of Knowledge and Other Essays, Brill, Leiden.

Von Wright G.H., (1997), "Progress: Fact and Fiction", in The Idea of Progress, ed. by A. Burgen et al., W. de Gruyter, Berlin, pp. 1-18.

Von Wright G.H., (1998), In the Shadow of Descartes: Essays in the Philosophy of Mind, Kluwer, Dordrecht.

Visalberghi E, Fragaszy D. (2002). Do monkeys ape? Ten years after. In: Dautenhahn K, Nehaniv C (eds) Imitation in animals and artifacts. MIT Press, Boston. Pp. 471–500

Weele C, Driessen C. (2016) In vitro meat is a chance to rethink. In: Stephens N, Kramer C, Denfeld Z,

Strand R (Hg). What is in vitro meat? Food Phreaking Issue 02: 57–59

Wicker B, Keysers C, Plailly J, Royet JP, Gallese V, Rizzolatti G (2003) Both of us disgusted in my insula: the common neural basis of seeing and feeling disgust. Neuron 40: 655–664.

Yokochi H, Tanaka M, Kumashiro M, Iriki A (2003) Inferior parietal somatosensory neurons coding face-hand coordination in Japanese macaques. Somatosens Mot Res 20 : 115–125.

Zald DH, Pardo JV (2000) Functional neuroimaging of the olfactory system in humans. Int J Psychophysiol 36: 165–181.

Zald DH, Donndelinger MJ, Pardo JV (1998) Elucidating dynamic brain interactions with across-subjects correlational analyses of positron emission tomographic data: the functional connectivity of the amygdala and orbitofrontal cortex during olfactory tasks. J Cereb Blood Flow Metab 18: 896–905.

OPERATION JUSTICE

OPERATION JUSTICE

OPERATION JUSTICE